PATRICK: A SAINT
(According to the ninth-century *Tripartite Life* of the Apostle of Ireland)

By the same author:

Ulster & Its Future After the Troubles (1977)
Ulster & The German Solution (1978)
Ulster & The British Connection (1979)
Ulster & The Lords of the North (1980)
Ulster & The Middle Ages (1982)
Ulster & St Patrick (1984)
The Twilight Pagans (1990)
Enemy of England (1991)
The Great Siege (2002)
Ulster in the Age of Saint Comgall of Bangor (2004)
Ulster Blood (2005)
King William's Victory (2006)
Ulster Stock (2007)
Famine in the Land of Ulster (2008)
Pre-Christian Ulster (2009)
The Glens of Antrim (2010)
Ulster Women – A Short History (2010)
The Invasion of Ulster (2010)
Ulster in the Viking Age (2011)
Ulster in the Eighteenth Century (2011)
Ulster in the History of Ireland (2012)
Rathlin Island (2013)
Saint Patrick's Missionary Journeys in Ireland (2015)
The Story of Carrickfergus (2015)
Ireland's Holy Places (2016)
The Conqueror of the North (2017)
The Story of Holywell Hospital: A Country Asylum (2018)

PATRICK: A SAINT FOR ALL SEASONS
(According to the ninth-century *Tripartite Life* of the Apostle of Ireland)

Michael Sheane

ARTHUR H. STOCKWELL LTD
Torrs Park, Ilfracombe, Devon, EX34 8BA
Established 1898
www.ahstockwell.co.uk

ISBN 978-0-7223-4920-5
Printed in Great Britain by
Arthur H. Stockwell Ltd
Torrs Park   Ilfracombe
Devon EX34 8BA

PATRICK: A SAINT FOR ALL SEASONS

(According to the ninth-century *Tripartite Life* of the Apostle of Ireland)

About the years AD 895–901 the *Bethu Patraic*, more widely known as *The Tripartite Life*, was written in Irish, so called because three monks wrote the book. Some historians believe that it follows the line of an earlier work, now lost to history. It is, however, beyond doubt that the stories in it are apocryphal. It is in *The Tripartite Life* that we find the claim that Patrick had his origins in Dumbarton in the west of Scotland. We learn that his mother was called Concessa. It records miracles about Patrick's birth, and attributes miraculous powers to him even in childhood. According to *The Tripartite Life* Patrick was baptized by a blind cleric called Gornias. Finding no water for the ceremony, Gornias made the sign of the cross with his hand, and water sprang up on the spot. When Gornias washed his face in the water, he was cured of his blindness; he was able to read the order of baptism even though he had never learnt to read.

The Tripartite Life assures readers that Patrick was endowed with great powers from his infancy. He was able to follow the way of truth – this in spite of Patrick's admission of youthful sins in his *Confession*, a mainly devotional work and declaration of faith. In *The*

Tripartite Life Patrick, a mere baby, saves people from a great flood. As a boy, playing with his foster-brother he brings him an icicle, breathes upon it and it begins to flare like timber. On another occasion he heals his sister Lupait when she falls and wounds her head on a stone.

When Patrick is blamed by his foster-mother for the loss of some sheep he was herding, which had been carried off by a wolf, the wolf comes to the house bringing a sheep, unharmed, in its jaws. He is recorded as having brought dead cattle back to life.

Patrick is attributed as having performed many other miracles and cures for diseases. When Patrick and his foster-mother are ordered to clean the hearth of the king's stronghold at Dumbarton, an angel appears and accomplishes this for him; the same king demands a tribute of butter and curds for Patrick's foster-mother. The lad performs many other miracles.

The Tripartite Life says that Patrick was not captured by Irish raiders, but by pirates from Brittany. Patrick's parents were slain by the pirates, and he was taken into captivity along with his two sisters, Lupait and Tigris. The pirates put out to sea, sailing northwards around the Irish coast, instead of heading for Brittany. Patrick, we are told, was sold as a slave to King Miliucc of Dalaradia or mid-Antrim; it is also possible that he was sold as a slave at the Larne market along with his sisters to another master. Patrick, we are told, served as a slave at Slemish Mountain for six or seven years. Here he had a vision of the Angel Victor. Patrick now instructed Miliucc in Christian precepts, which he accepted.

The account of Patrick's escape from Slemish tallies with other accounts, but *The Tripartite Life* says that the boat in which Patrick sailed took him to Brittany. On his way to the continent, to Italy, he met St Germanus. Patrick, aged thirty, decided to stay with Germanus at Auxerre. He made his way to Tours to be tonsured in the monastic foundation of St Martin. Patrick stayed in Europe for thirty years, which time he spent in the island monastery of Lerins.

It was in France or Gaul that Patrick was visited by the Angel Victor, who commanded him to go to Ireland to bring the word. With a party of nine evangelists he set out for Ireland, sailing no doubt from a Mediterranean port for France, travelling via the Straits of Gibraltar, around the Iberian Peninsula and across the Bay of Biscay to the south of Ireland, but some believe that he may have reached the Holy Land first rather than sailing directly to Erin. We learn that Patrick was in possession of the Baculus Jesu, a relic of Christ's staff, which was venerated in Ireland until its destruction at the time of the Reformation.

Patrick went to Mount Hermon, where God appeared to him to tell him to go forth and preach to the Gaels. Patrick travelled to Rome to be received by Pope Celestine, where he was ordained.

At length Patrick and his missionaries arrived in Ireland; they reached the River Vartry, where Patrick started to convert the Gaels, this happening in the fifth year of the reign of the High King Leoghaire, who had bowed down to idols.

From the mouth of the Vartry, Patrick sailed northwards to arrive at Maladhide, and from here he continued to Inishpatrick, then on to the River Boyne. When a wizard mocked the Virgin Mary, Patrick made the sign of the cross, and the wizard was swallowed up by the Earth. Patrick had hidden his boats on the bank of the River Slaney, County Down; now he baptized Dichu – the local king, – and received from him a barn in which to set up his first church in Ireland. Patrick went forth to meet up with his former slave master (which implies that Patrick may have been given his freedom by Miliucc), but upon hearing of Patrick's coming he committed suicide, burning himself.

Now Patrick returned to Dichu's court in Ulidia to perform more conversions; he tonsured his converts. Then Patrick decided to celebrate Easter in the vicinity of Tara. He lit the Paschal fire on the Hill of Slane. At Slane, where the deer were seen to flee, *The Tripartite Life* puts into the Saint's mouth words of exaltation, better known as St Patrick's Breastplate. Patrick prophesied that three great saints would come into existence: Columba, Comgall and Finnian. From Tara Patrick went to Teltown in County Meath, the site of Celtic assemblies and games which took place annually in August. Today a number of remains can be seen, spread over a large area; the centre appears to have been Rath Dubh, the Black Fort, a circular earthwork about 150 feet in diameter and partly surrounded by a bawn. Cremated bones have been discovered in a field, indicating that it was a cemetery in pre-Christian times. After further conversions Patrick returned to Tara, where the High King Leoghaire told of his difficulty in believing the new faith.

It is also stated that Patrick visited Rome on three occasions during his mission to Ireland.

We are told that Patrick met a woman called Tigel, whose son was ill, and Patrick blessed her. The boy learnt the Psalms in twelve days. Here Patrick may have set up other churches, falling under the paruchia, or monastic sphere, of Clonmacnoise, and subsequently that of Clonard.

In Meath the Saint came to the Tech Laisren, where he performed many baptisms. Travelling south, the Saint founded a church on the shores of Lough Endell. There were two other foundations in this region, but they cannot easily be identified.

Patrick set out on another expedition from Tara to Uisneach, County Westmeath, on a fertile plain called Teachba, which was the granary of Ireland. It was not only a royal site, but also the headquarters of a great assembly in Erin. The great gathering took place on May Day (Beltane). A number of remains can still be seen on the hill, including the remains of a fort. The stone remains on Ail Na Meeran (the Stone of Divinity) on the western side of the Hill of Uisneach are believed to mark the spot where the five great provinces of Ireland converge. We are told that what Emain Macha was to Ulster, Tara to Meath, Cruachan to Connaught and Cashel to Munster, Uisneach was to Westmeath.

Enda, the High King, received the missionary message. *The Tripartite Life* goes on to relate that the baptism took place in County Westmeath. Enda gave Patrick one-ninth of his land, and offered his newborn son to the Saint. With other followers Patrick left the holy relics at Leckan, County Westmeath.

Patrick now crossed the River Shannon at a ford named Twin Birds. This was before there were bridges on the river, so the crossing had to be made where the water was shallow. Where Patrick crossed the Shannon is a mystery. It is said that Patrick's charioteer died at the ford. According to local tradition, Patrick blessed the ford, so no one ever again drowned there despite the strong currents. Once across the Shannon, Patrick informed his disciples of the underground altar with glass chalices at its four angles, but no explanation is given for the existence of this piece of church furniture. At Kilmore, County Roscommon, on the plain of Moyglass Patrick placed some of his followers to oversee the church that he had founded in the region. He came across more wizards, Id and Hono. Hono rejected the gift of eternal life which Patrick offered to him in payment for his land, but he accepted a lump of gold which the Saint found where swine were rooting nearby. At Elphin, also in Roscommon, Patrick dug a well and established a foundation nearby; he left in charge of it a bishop named Erc the Red, who offered the Saint his dwelling. This foundation was shortly followed by another at Shankhill, also in Roscommon, where he left some disciples at a dun.

After his next foundation, at Tawney, County Sligo, Patrick arrived at the Well of Clebach beside Rathcroghan where *The Tripartite Life* records the conversion of Leoghaire's daughters, which agrees with other works. *The Tripartite Life* names the next foundations at Ardleckna and other places, again in County Roscommon, before bringing the Saint to Fuerty, where his Frankish disciples left him to continue to convert the Gaels; here he founded the church at Oran. Next we find Patrick in the vicinity of Tulsk, still in Roscommon, at the Mound of the Chase, where he wrote on three stones – 'Jesus', 'Sotor' and 'Salvator'.

On the southern shore of Lough Gara Patrick founded

another church, and beside it he dug a well, which was reputed to never run dry although no streams fed it. He now founded a number of convents, and hospitals existed near them until the sixteenth-century Reformation.

After pursuing the sons of Erco, who stole his horse, Patrick reached the Barony of Costello in County Mayo, where another well was established. Patrick now foiled an attempt upon his life, and he retired into the wilderness for two Sundays. In County Mayo he left a bishop named Decnach to care for the foundation. Here Patrick put two salmon into the well which he said would live for ever. On the Saturday after Shrovetide the great height of the Twelve Pins of Connemara, and the 130 islets of Clew Bay, could be seen from as far away as Donegal. On the top of Croagh Patrick the saint wrestled with an angel who appeared to him, saying that he was making unreasonable demands. Discouraged, Patrick reached Croagh Patrick and from Shrove Saturday until Easter Sunday he abstained from both food and drink. God had spoken to Patrick out of a fire.

At the end of forty days and nights a vast swirl of blackbirds covered the plain where Patrick was, so that he could not see. Patrick wept copiously; the angel tried to console him, drying the tears on his chasuble (an item of clothing). White birds could be seen flying over the area of Croagh Patrick, and the angel promised him the sea and land as far as his eyes could see. The angel told Patrick that he might have saved seven souls from hell every Saturday until Doomsday. Patrick replied that he would like it to be twelve souls, but the angel was not impressed. The angel said that he would grant his request if he would leave the mountain, or reek. The angel revealed that a great flood would engulf Erin seven years before Judgement Day, and Patrick said that he would not leave the reek. The angel asked him if he had any further demands and Patrick said that he had. Patrick said that it was his right to dwell in Ireland. The angel promised relief from any pain for those who would sing the Saint's hymn from one watch to another. The angel said that Patrick should leave the mountain at once, saying that he would not accept this blessing.

The angel cried out to Patrick that he was stressing matters if he refused to obey the will of God. The Saint boldly cried out that the High King supported him and that it was the will of the Pope that he should evangelize Ireland and save souls from purgatory and hell. The Saint said that on Judgement Day he would sit in judgement over the people of Ireland, but the angel said that this would not be possible. Patrick said that there was no way he would leave the mountain by Doomsday.

The angel went back to heaven, and Patrick celebrated Mass or Holy Communion. The angel retired at the ninth hour to relay to Patrick God's message. The Saint celebrated Easter at Aughagower, and his charioteer was buried in the region between the mountains and the sea. He founded three churches at Partry, County Mayo, and baptized many more there. He was told that there was an important pagan well, the King of Waters, so he and his neophyte Cannech, the founder Bishop of Cara, County Mayo, removed the stone that covered the well. We learn that Patrick brought back to life a pagan that had died 100 years earlier. The victim cried out that he was a wretched heathen. At the sign of the cross Patrick had brought the pagan back to life.

Patrick now crossed the River Moy to Tirawley, County Mayo, where the twelve sons of Amalgaid were fighting over the High Kingship. They set out for Tara in their chariots so that Leoghaire could judge the issue. The Saint wanted to convert more pagans, so he set up the Catholic Church in Ireland. But Patrick had enemies, and he expected that he would become the victim of religious as well as pagan foes. He said prayers for the establishment of the Kingdom of God. The pagans held strong at Killala, County Mayo, along with the magicians. *The Tripartite Life* records that the spot where there was a wizard's stone should be named Cross Padraigh.

Ruan, the blind son of Amalgaid's charioteer, came to Patrick in order to be healed. When one of Patrick's followers laughed at the charioteer, Patrick cured the blind man. Others were also healed, including a lame man. Still in the neighbourhood of Killala, near the well of Cross Patrick, one Aed, a grandson of Oengus, was healed of leprosy by the Saint. The evil was consumed in heaven's fire. However, it is difficult to pinpoint the precise locations of Patrick's healing endeavours. Patrick brought with him his two sisters, who had prayed for the success of his mission to the Gaels, again according to *The Tripartite Life*. But one of Amalgaid's sons, Oengus, had seen Fedelem brought back to life. Two others of the people of amadain of the Forest of Foclut now believed in Christ.

Oengus owned land in the neighbourhood of the necropolis of Loughdall, and Patrick went there with the expectation that he would be given land, upon which he would set up a foundation. But Oengus was a superficial fellow – when he met Patrick he was under the influence of the drink or poteen. Patrick now told him that all his relations would be drunkards and parricides. At Kilmoremoy in County Mayo (and in County Sligo) the Saint erected a stone cross, and here he performed many other miracles, including resurrecting a man's dead wife from the grave.

Near the banks of the River Moy are the ruins of two Franciscan friaries, Moyne and Rosserk. Patrick soon inspired his followers, and the Saint declared that they should never be subjected to stress and they would always be able to meet in assembly. On his way into the tribal territory of the Ui Frachrach Patrick cursed a flood which impeded his progress. *The Tripartite Life* says that in his day a flagstone marked the spot where Patrick performed many miracles; the stone is now in the National Museum of Ireland, Dublin.

In County Sligo three fishermen talked with Patrick, and the Saint reassured them that Christianity was for them. He told the fishermen to cast their nets into the river.

In County Roscommon he fell into the River Boyle, and he cursed it.

There was also the prospect of obtaining a little fruit. The Saint went to County Leitrim, where he performed more miracles, and he founded another church. Crossing the plain, Patrick blessed the River Drowes as a result of the kindness shown to him by the fishermen.

At Assaroe, in County Donegal, the local magnates wanted to expel Patrick, but they were unsuccessful, and a dog was set on the Saint. Another church was founded at Racoo, near Ballyshannon, and Patrick prophesied that the princely seat would be his. *The Tripartite Life* also foretells the coming of Columba (sixth century).

Now Patrick passed through the Gap of Barnesmore, with mountains on either side; here he founded another church and formed a relationship with the chief, Eogan, son of Niall. One of Eogan's sons, Muiredach, was converted to the faith and he obtained a kingship as a result. Eogan came to the Saint and said he believed in Christ.

Patrick headed for Inishbofin, the land of W. B. Yeats. Patrick covered Eogan and Rioc with a mantle, and they fell asleep, clasping each other's arms. Patrick blessed Eogan and his followers. They were rewarded with kingships, and some of them were to become priests; the heirs of Eochu were to be warriors.

Patrick now came to Ailech in County Donegal to the great stronghold there, seat of the Ui Neill clan, or tribe, in the fifth century. It commanded a great view over Lough Swilly and Lough Foyle. The concentric stone ramparts still remain. The enclosures of the area are seventy-seven feet in diameter; the walls are no less than thirteen feet thick, containing chambers in the masonry. *The Tripartite Life* records that Patrick gave his blessing to the fortress, and he made prophecies and blessed the native tribes. After blessing all the Inishowen Peninsula as far as Malin Head, Patrick founded seven churches along the River Faughan. Only three are identifiable: at Clooney in County Londonderry, and at Bodoney and Donaghead in County Tyrone.

The Saint returned to Inishowen, where just west of Moville a lane climbs up to Cooley, where there is a stone cross, ten feet high. The local tradition has it that there were important footprints of the Saint in the stones, but *The Tripartite Life* says that he returned to County Tyrone; Patrick ordained three bishops there, and seven churches were established in the Barony of Keenaght. Patrick came across the local rí, or king, where it was the tradition of the inhabitants to feast by night, but Patrick said that they should eat by day. He travelled widely in both Dalaradia and Dalriada, receiving land from the local kings.

A local tradition tells that Patrick came across an infant whom he wanted to baptize, but the ground opened up and odours of stale wine poured forth. In the vicinity was a woman who had died of ague; Patrick blessed her, and her infant lived on after her death, having been in the tomb for seven days. Patrick baptized the child, the future Bishop Olcan of County Antrim. Patrick set up churches and cloisters at Romoan, at Culeightrim, at Grange and at Drumeeny. Dunseverick, on the north coast, was an embarkation port for Scotland. Patrick blessed the place and established a well. He founded more churches and monasteries. But he cursed Saran, who he said would perhaps go to hell. Land was offered to Patrick at Comber in County Down, and he converted the kings' people as he made his progress through Ireland.

Other Patrician sites in County Antrim are on the Island Magee peninsula, between Lough Larne and the sea, at Rashee in the Barony of Upper Antrim, at Glore in Glenarm and in the Barony of Lower Belfast. Sites at Larne are believed to be the locations of other churches and oratories in the little valleys and hills, where they could get close to God.

Next *The Tripartite Life* tells how Olcan, already a bishop, pleaded for the liberty of the captive held by Patrick's adversary Saran at Glenavey. In return for his freedom, Olcan and the Saint met a few miles north of the city of Armagh, where Patrick ordered his charioteer to drive right over Olcan, hoping to save their lives, invoking the spirit of God. Patrick cured a monk who was losing his faith, and he said that the victim should go on to become a bishop. The Saint cursed the monk's earthly goods, but also told him that he would be exalted in heaven. But grief was the penalty that the unfortunate Olcan had to experience.

A brother of Saran's received a site at Coleraine in County Londonderry for Patrick. The Saint foretold that this foundation would belong to both him and a donor, this being at last fulfilled by the person of Carther, the donor's grandson, consecrated by a bishop who had been consecrated by Patrick.

Patrick brought him out of Dalaradia or mid-Antrim, with Guasacht and the two relations – the son and daughter of King Miliucc, his former slave master – when he was tending sheep around Slemish Mountain in the fifth century. He left the kingdom by way of Toomebridge, where the River Bann flows out of Lough Neagh. The village today is the largest eel fishery in the British Isles, managed by a cooperative of about 400 local fishermen and farmers.

The Saint received land from the Ui Tuirtri, where he remained for forty days at a spot between the lough and Slieve Gullion, which has been called Ireland's most mysterious mountain. Patrick wished to found a cloister there, but he was opposed by the local ruler, who ordered Patrick to leave. The Saint converted his adversary and deprived him of his territory in favour of the ruler's brother, who along with his wife was blessed and baptized. She gave birth to a daughter, Trea. She became a nun, and an angel brought a veil for her from heaven. Patrick blessed the veil and wished her a long life.

Seven churches founded by Patrick in the lands of the Ui Tuitri are named in *The Tripartite Life*, and four can be identified. One is at Dunaghurst, a foundation in the Upper Barony, County Tyrone, and the other is at Dunshaughlin in the same county. There were hostile tribes that lay to the west of Dungannon receiving Patrick's message, and he blessed and baptized the men of another tribe in the same vicinity; he left the priest Columba there and also a bell.

After visiting Tullamain in County Londonderry, the Saint turned south to found churches and cloisters in the Barony of Slain, County Meath. From there it appears that Patrick returned to what is now the road to Clogher in County Tyrone with his disciples, one of which became a bishop there. Clogher is still the seat of a bishop, and although now little remains of the village it is proud of its ancient history, and tradition holds that it was founded by Patrick.

The Protestant church at Clogher is dedicated to St Macartan, the first bishop there. We know that in Patrick's day Clogher was a place of much importance, for there are Roman remains. Excavations on the hill fort of Rathmore date back to the Iron Age. The Saint left at Clogher a relic called the Domhnach Airgid, which he had received when he was on his way from Rome to Ireland.

On a hill at Findermore is a foundation in the Barony of Clogher. Patrick preached for three days and three nights. Bridget, had fallen asleep during a long sermon, and Patrick did not confront her. He later asked her what she had seen, and Bridget told Patrick that she had seen an assembly of people all robed in white, with light-coloured oxen and oxen of other colours. Patrick tried to change his attitude to Bridget. The two sons of Echaid opposed the Saint, but Patrick cursed them.

The next evening Cinnu came, the daughter of a ruler named Echu, whom Patrick raised from the dead. Cinnu was a baptized believer and she had heard from Patrick the joy of the spirit – she was to be wed to the heavenly Bridegroom. Patrick exhorted Echu to let Cinnu become a nun. Echu hesitated, but gave his consent to obtain heaven as the result of good works. Now Cinnu took the veil, joined the Saint's retinue and was sent to a cloister to be instructed in the faith.

Echu was coming near the end of his life, and he told those who were with him to bring the Saint; and as soon as he said this he died. Patrick was at Saul, in County Down, when he heard news of this. He set out for Clogher about twenty-four hours later. It was a scene rather like those in the New Testament, for the Saint had performed many miracles, perhaps turning stone into bread and water into wine. He had entered the house of a believer who had died, and raised the body.

Falling to his knees, Patrick wept and prayed, and then called Echu in the name of God to arise; he sat down and spoke. The mourners cried out, and Patrick instructed Echu in the faith, and baptized him. The Saint instructed people on the pains of hell and the joys of heaven. Patrick took into account Echu's royal person. Echu replied that even though the kingship should be granted to him, he had to accept the doctrines and dogmas of the Catholic Church, for he had set up the primatial see at Armagh in AD 455. He was a companion to the Saint and watched his master teach the doctrine of the Trinity in the fields of Ulster and afar. Patrick was a man of sorrows, but firm in the Catholic faith, a believer in the power of Mary to heal sinners and to raise them from the dead.

At Tehalilan in the Barony of Monaghan, Patrick left a bishop and some aged disciples.

Three men stole some of the goats that belonged to the Saint, killing and eating them. Patrick questioned them, but a goat bleated in their bellies. He cursed the thieves.

Now the King of Omeath, whom Patrick had blessed and baptized, blessed the inhabitants. Patrick tried to reassure him about his dead grandfather, Muiredach, who was brought back from the dead and baptized.

In the Barony of Cromore, County Monaghan, was a man named Victor. Upon hearing of Patrick's arrival he had lit a thicket, miraculously illuminated at night. Victor now submitted himself to Patrick and became a real believer.

Still in the Barony of Farney, Patrick performed more miracles, and two miles from Carrickmacross he established further churches. The people of the place provided Patrick with poisoned cheese to eat, but Patrick blessed the cheese and it was turned into stone. *The Tripartite Life* asserts that the stones could still be seen at the place.

Patrick travelled post-haste with a band of horses, for people were out to get him in the pagan world. The Saint raised his hand and made the sign of the cross, saying that they would all be drowned in the waters until the coming of Domesday. They waded into the waters, which swept across them and they were drowned.

At Coole, in County Meath, Patrick blessed the inhabitants and set up a foundation which was subsequently like the churches at Dunmurraghill, County Kildare. He also went to Naas, where he met the local king and chiefs on the green overlooking the fort capital; he baptized his neophytes in the waters to the north of the dun, or fort. Patrick summoned the reeve of the fort, but he feigned sleep. When Patrick was told, he exclaimed that it did not surprise him. When the reeve's men returned to the fort to awaken him, they found him dead.

After Naas the Saint reached County Wicklow, where he was refused permission to attend a feast. But Patrick was welcomed by another of the Ui Garrchon, who killed his only cow and gave him his share. The man's pregnant wife believed Patrick, who blessed the couple and their unborn child.

Patrick now founded a church and cloister on the plain of the River Liffey, at Killashee, where he left Iserninis and other disciples.

On the Saint's route westwards, young boys from Leix laid a trap for him – concrete pits filled with water – at Moone in County Kildare. When he reached the place, the boys urged him to drive on. Patrick ordered his charioteer to hurry on, and the Saint was left unharmed; he laid a curse on the people of Leix. Since a woman of the Ui Ercain named Brig had informed the Saint of the trap, Patrick blessed her and upheld her independence.

At a church not far from Sletty in County Leix Patrick

asked Dubthach maccu Lugair for a comely well-born young man with only one wife who had not yet had a child. Dubthach replied that unfortunately the young man was away in Connaught. Patrick blessed him, and once he was baptized, tonsured and made Bishop of Leinster, Patrick presented Dubthach with a bell, crozier and other sacred objects, and he left seven of his disciples to settle in a foundation two miles from what is today in County Carlow; there were also thirty or forty other churches founded in Leinster that had been donated by Patrick's relations along with the Magnate Cremthan.

Fiacc's original foundation was on the east side of the River Barrow; but after an angel had appeared to him, Patrick was sure that his own church at Sletty would flourish. The monastery of Sletty was plundered in the ninth century, and it also survived later attacks; the last Abbot of Sletty was Maelbrighide, who died in 1055. Little is left of the monastery, but there are remains which appear to date from the early-Church period, and there are also medieval traces.

On Sundays, when Patrick established a church on the plain near Morett, County Leix, the Saint forbade some workmen to dig for a feast on the sabbath. But they did not heed him; Patrick foretold that unless the sacrifice of the Mass was offered every day the stronghold would be unstable.

Patrick's route took him through the Gowran Pass in Ossory, where he founded a church and a cloister. At Kells, in County Kildare, there are the ruins of an Augustinian priory, where Patrick left some relatives in the care of the disciples who remained there. On his way into Munster the axle of Patrick's chariot broke; two others followed suit. Patrick decided that no building made out of wood would take place in the area as a result. *The Tripartite Life* tells us that his prophecies in regard to this would be fulfilled.

When Patrick reached the Rock of Cashel, in County Tipperary, the local king, Oengus, awoke in the morning to find all his idols had been knocked down. At this, the sons of Natfraich were baptized by the Saint, and he blessed the men of Munster. When Patrick baptized Oengus the spike of his crozier fell on the King's foot; but the King did not complain. Patrick told Oengus that he was an upright Christian convert. *The Tripartite Life* records that twenty-seven king-bishops of the family of Oengus would rule Cashel until the accession of one Cenngecan, a king-bishop of Cashel who was slain in AD 897.

The Rock of Cashel rises from the surrounding plains, and it was an important site before Patrick's mission to Erin. It had been fortified by the King of Munster since the fourth century; it was also the scene of many historic happenings. The famous High King Brian Boru was crowned on the Rock of Cashel in AD 977. The King Muirchertach O'Brian gave the rock to the Church in 1101. The king-bishop Cairn MacCarthy built the lovely Romanesque church on the rock; it was consecrated in 1134. The round tower is from about the same date, and the ruined castle was dedicated to St Patrick, most likely in the thirteenth century.

The conversion of the High King of Munster was a great achievement for Patrick – the highlight of his career. According to *The Tripartite Life*, Patrick remained in Munster for seven years. From Cashel he went on to found churches and cloisters in County Tipperary.

When he was out wading into a river, one of his teeth fell out and fell into the river; he sent some of his followers to search after it. It reflected the light of the sun. The place was named Ath Fiacla (the Ford of the Tooth). With four of his disciples he waded again into the river, so the place was named the Ford of the Foot.

Patrick reached County Limerick, and he travelled to the lovely Glen of Aherlow with its scenic hills around Galbach. Despite the opposition of the local magnates, Cobre and Broccan, he eventually received a place to set up a church. Another magnate, Dola, also opposed Patrick in his desire to sojourn at his foundation near Pallas Grean. Dola had a firm religious faith. In the plains to the west all but two or three people lived in slavery or wretchedness and many of the others would emigrate. Patrick's message of the faith now extended into the realm of children, whom he was anxious to convert for the future of the Church. This would also be extended to the other tribes or *tuatha*, other than Dola's.

Patrick was establishing a church on a hill in the Barony of Coonagh at Kilteely, where he found two slaves asleep; and the two are buried there. The hill was known as Cromwell Hill. It rises to about 580 feet and commands an extensive view over the River Shannon and its valley. On its summit is a prehistoric burial cairn known as Diarmuid and Grainne's Bed. Patrick continued into the territory of the Ui Fidgente, where a banquet was prepared for him.

The annals record the death date for St Nessan of Mungret as AD 551. It is said that he lived until he was eighty, so he would have been a young man during St Patrick's mission to the Gaels of Ireland. The monastery there flourished and it is said that the community numbered 1,600; it survived the Danish attacks in the ninth century, but it was plundered by the Gaelic chiefs. The ruins of an early church must have been on the site of this ancient foundation.

The men of Munster who came by ship to meet Patrick were baptized. He blessed them for their generosity on a hilltop that commanded a good view of the surrounding hills to the north of Leinster. The peak, of volcanic origin, has been called Knockpatrick, with views over the River Shannon and its valley. The Saint blessed the lands around Limerick and the islands in the Shannon Estuary. He did not go west into the mountains, but went south into the land of Coshlea to found a church at a place called Ardpatrick, County Limerick. Here the local magnate, Derball, had come by the Ballyhoura Mountains so that he would be able to see as far as the Barony of Fermoy. Derball said that he would embrace Christianity if the Saint performed miracles to combat paganism. The mountains are quite visible from the River Shannon.

Upon reaching the River Suir, Patrick blessed it and prayed that the lands would be fruitful. He evangelized in the Barony of Lower and Upper Ormond, where he raised a man from the dead, the man having been dead for some time. When the Saint eventually left the province of Munster, after founding churches and cloisters, he performed ordinations, healing the sick and raising the dead. He and his followers, men, women and children, reached Brosna in County Offaly. At Brosna he resurrected a man who had been dead for twenty-seven years. Patrick's followers in Munster attended a feast, which he blessed, at Creevagh, County Offaly, and there he performed a number of benedictions; he then bade them farewell.

From Creevagh, Patrick's itinerary took him to the lands of the Ui Falgi, a region on the eastern side of the lands in the Barony of Offaly in County Kildare. There a devotee of the idol Crom Cruach, Ireland's national idol, boasted that he would kill the Saint in revenge for overturning the idol, which stood on a plain in County Cavan. However, Patrick's charioteer defended his master, saying that the overturning of the idol was an act of God. The pagans were cursed, died, and went at once to hell.

Patrick returned to Ulster and encountered on his way some slaves who were in the process of felling some trees. To make them suffer more they were not even allowed to sharpen their tools, so they had bled from their exertions. Patrick went to one of the slaves and pleaded for him, but to no avail. He cursed the slave owner and the pagan was filled with fear. The master's widow was told by Patrick to repent and kneel before him; he then blessed her womb and her two sons were baptized. Patrick predicted that her son Iarlaith would be one of her successors.

One Sunday when Patrick was sleeping near the sea on a plain called Drumbo he was disturbed by the voices of pagans digging at a rath. He asked them to stop the noise, but they ignored him. The Saint predicted that their efforts would be for naught. The prediction soon proved to be true. The next night there was a storm, and the sea came up and demolished the earthen structure. Echaid bade the two maidens to leave the strand to be washed over by the sea, for they had vowed to behold the idols. Echaid then entreated Patrick on behalf of the girls, so the Saint cursed them and the kingship passed to the descendants of Echaid's brother. But Echaid's pregnant wife received Patrick's blessing, and he blessed the unborn child.

At Drumcar in the Barony of Ardee, County Louth, an angel told Patrick not to construct a cloister which he was planning to build there. The angel told the Saint that Armagh was to be the site of the primatial see. Patrick looked at the nearby meadow, and the angel told him that it would be called the Fair Meadow, and that British pilgrims would come and establish a foundation there. There was a monastery in the region until the latter years of the ninth century.

At Ardpatrick, County Louth, where he wanted to establish a foundation, an angel told him to found a cloister. Patrick blessed the people along with his followers. Each day he went to the meadow with his disciple Mochtae at a place between Ardpatrick and his other foundations in County Louth, where an early church still stands. One day another angel placed a letter between them, telling Mochtae to remain at his own foundation and to proceed to Armagh or Ard Macha.

Patrick travelled to Armagh at the angel's bidding, and he arrived at the rath of a rich magnate and asked him for a site for a church. He was not given the hill that he asked for (the present site of the Protestant cathedral), but another site. The Saint spent some time at Armagh. One day the magnate sent two of his horses to graze on church lands, but Patrick was enraged and the horses died at once. The magnate said that the horses had been killed. He asked if Patrick should be driven out, but the chief fell ill. His wife, who also wished to expel the Saint, told her husband that the illness was due to the treatment given him by Patrick, and here she asked for holy water for her husband. Because of the wife's faith, Patrick sent the holy water, which was sprinkled over the chief, and he was restored to life and health.

The grateful chief sent Patrick a copper cauldron. Later Ercnat, a daughter of the chief, fell in love with one of Patrick's disciples, Benignus, but she died. Benignus took her to Patrick, and he resurrected Ercnat, who offered love to Benignus both physically and spiritually. Now ten people in the province of Ulster, the King of Louth and one of the kings of Britain came on a pilgrimage to Patrick. They rested at Armagh and sent messengers to Patrick. He said that three of them would go to heaven and would be buried on the spot where they had stood, to be afterwards known as Druim Fendeda. One of the foundations, on a certain hill at Cengoba, lay east of Armagh. Every night Benignus took food on Patrick's instructions. One Cruimthens had a lapdog which drank doe's milk. Patrick had an apple tree transplanted, and the field thereafter was known as Patrick's Orchard.

Patrick rested one night by a well, and the angel awakened him. Patrick asked the angel if he had given any offerings to God. The angel said that he had not and that Patrick would succeed to spiritual dominion in Erin. Patrick replied that he would like them to succeed for the sake of the Kingdom of Heaven. At this Patrick was informed that his sister Lupait had been guilty of the sin of lust, for now she was pregnant.

The authors of *The Tripartite Life* recorded the chronology of Patrick's life, and it relates that his sister had become abandoned because of her sin. Patrick of course was aware that she was pregnant at a time when he had been conducting his mission in Ireland for some years. We are told that Lupait would be flung under the Saint's chariot, and Patrick commanded that this should be so. Her remains were interred with a requiem Mass. Lupait had pleaded with Patrick, for he was aware that she had sexual intercourse with her lover and she would shortly be giving birth. The Saint granted Lupait's request for forgiveness so that she would go to heaven, but he said that they would also feel sickly. At a place where an angel removed a stone out of the way of Patrick's chariot he raised his hand and blessed Armagh, holding the Baculus Jesu. Patrick surveyed the enclosure that the chief had given him, presumably at Armagh. He pronounced a curse on these pagans and blessed all that would do God's work. Now he measured the length of the burial ground, the great house (140 feet), the kitchen (twenty-seven feet) and the oratory (seven feet). We are told that they were the standard measurements of Patrick's institutions while he was converting the pagan Gaels.

The remains of Emain Macha, ancient Ulster's capital, lie two miles to the west of Armagh, and today, as in Patrick's time, consist of an earthwork and a low line of drumlins. According to *The Tripartite Life* it was at Armagh that God appeared to the Saint. Patrick was so overawed that he fled to the south of Ireland. The relics kept at Armagh are explained by a journey taken by Patrick to Rome that he undertook from Ireland in a boat that had come to fetch him from Bordeaux. With God's blessing Patrick brought 165 relics to Armagh, including relics of Peter, Paul, Lawrence and Stephen, a sheet of Christ's stained blood and a hair of the Virgin Mary. A load of wheat from heaven was brought to Patrick. He sent horses yoked to a chariot from Armagh to Fiacc at Sletty. The horses reached Mochtae's foundation at Louth, where they made their way by ship. Then they made their way into County Meath and County Kildare.

One Sechnall asked Patrick which hymn he would sing, but he did not think that this was a good idea. Patrick learnt that Sechnall was an excellent man. A religious couple brought butter and cheese made out of curds for the young boys in the country.

A wizard told Patrick that if he turned stone into cheese he would believe in Christ, and Patrick achieved this. The wizard then asked Patrick to change the cheese back into stone once again, and Patrick complied. The wizard asked again for the miracle to be performed, but this time the Saint refused, and said that the stone should remain as a commemoration of the miracle. The wizard became a convert to the faith.

When the hour of death was approaching, Patrick came to Armagh to die and be buried there. The Angel Victor appeared to him and told him that Armagh was not the place appointed for him to pass on; the angel told him to head for County Down, where he should end his days. The angel instructed Patrick on where he should be buried: he was to be drawn by oxen in a cart, and where the oxen stopped would be the place of his burial. *The Tripartite Life* records that his body was put on a cart and driven to Downpatrick, where he was buried without ceremony. For twelve nights after his death, the whole of the kingdom of Lecale was lit up in a radiance. Some accounts state that the radiance lasted for about a year after his passing. The Ulidians, the Ui Neill and the men of Donegal competed for Patrick's body.

Between sixty and seventy books about St Patrick are known to have existed in pre-Viking Ireland, but these were destroyed by the raiders who had come from Scandinavia. By the twelfth century, Jocelin of Furness wrote *The Life of Patrick*, and the legends about Patrick were in full growth. Further deeds were attributed to the Saint, chiefly mentioning holy wells. Information about the life of the Saint was widely circulated. It was in the late twelfth century that a legend about the Saint materialized, for he had taken himself to Lough Derg in County Donegal to found what is known today as St Patrick's Purgatory. The first modern account of Patrick's life was written by Richard Stanihurst, and published in Antwerp in 1587. O'Sullevan Beare's *Patriciana Decas* was published in 1629. The first critical account of the Saint was written by James Ussher when he was Primate of All Ireland in 1639. For about 200 years Ussher's work was the only reliable work on the Saint. In the nineteenth century (1864) *St Patrick, Apostle of Ireland* appeared. Another work, *The Life of St Patrick*, was published in Irish in 1905; *The Story of Saint Patrick* was also written by Father Gaffney, who portrayed Patrick as a national hero. By the twentieth century some historians believed that Patrick did not exist. However, the historian J. B. Bury put forward the theory that Patrick was born at Dumbarton in Scotland, and that he did exist; another work, *The Life and Legend of Saint Patrick*, was published in 1949. In this biography Patrick appears as a real person, though modern criticism supports the view that St Patrick may not have been a real person. However, there are, as we have seen, a number of works about the Saint. There are his own works – the *Confession* and the letter to Coroticus – outlining his beliefs, and other works written shortly after his death; also the books of the medieval historians.

Today Patrick is the world's most celebrated saint. In Belfast, Dublin and abroad, as far away as the United States, a pint of Guinness is drunk to the health of the Apostle of Ireland. It is certain that the legend of the Saint will last for many centuries beyond the present one.

Of modern works telling the story of the Saint, one may read *In the Steps of St Patrick* by Brian de Breffny, 1982. But perhaps Bury's account will be the more long-lasting. Today in Ireland, both north and south, many churches have been dedicated to St Patrick, along with Christ's mother, the Virgin Mary.

SELECT BIBLIOGRAPHY

A. B. E. Hood (editor), *St Patrick* (Phillimore).

Brian de Breffny, *In the Steps of St Patrick* (Thames & Hudson, 1982).

Cormac Bourke, *Patrick, the Archaeology of a Saint* (HMSO, Belfast, 1993).

I. J. Herring, *History of Ireland* (W. H. Mullan & Sons, 1951).

James Carney, *Historical Memoirs of the Problem of St Patrick* (Dublin Institute of Advanced Studies, 1973).

James Stuart, *Historical Memoirs of the City of Armagh* (Brown & Nolan, 1900).

Lesley Whiteside, Saint *Patrick in Stained Glass* (Gill & Macmillan, 1997).

Maureen Donnelly, *St Patrick & the Downpatrick Area* (the author, 1995).

Michael Sheane, *Saint Patrick's Missionary Journeys in Ireland* (Arthur H. Stockwell Ltd, 2015).

Michael Sheane, *Ulster & St Patrick* (Highfield Press, 1984).

P. W. Joyce, *A Concise History of Ireland* (The Educational Company of Ireland).